High-Tech DIY Projects with Microcontrollers

Maggie Murphy

PowerKiDS press

New York

Published in 2015 by The Rosen Publishing Group, Inc.
29 East 21st Street, New York, NY 10010

First Edition

Editors: Jennifer Way and Jacob Seifert
Book Design: Andrew Povolny
Photo Research: Katie Stryker

Photo Credits: Cover Arthur Dries/Taxi/Getty Images; p. 4 Kameel4u/Shutterstock.com; p. 5 anaken2012/Shutterstock.com; p. 6 Westebd61/Brand X Pictures/Getty Images; p. 7 Evan Sharboneau/Hemera/Thinkstock; p. 8 Yamini Chao/Digital Vision/Thinkstock; p. 9 Creatas Images/Thinkstock; p. 10 Tim Ridley/Dorling Kindersley/Getty Images; p. 11 Luna Vandoome/Shutterstock; p. 12 Jupiter Images/Photolibrary/Getty Images; pp. 13, 15 Fuse/Thinkstock; pp. 16–19 littleBits; pp. 24 (top/bottom), 25 (top/bottom) Katie Stryker; pp. 20–21, 22 c.d. stone; p. 23 theJIPEN/iStock/Thinkstock; p. 25 © Arduino; p. 26 Bloomburg/Getty Images; p. 27 Visuals Unlimited Inc/GIPhotoStock/Getty Images; p. 28 Jupiterimages/Creatas/Thinkstock; p. 29 Monkey Business Images/Thinkstock.

Library of Congress Cataloging-in-Publication Data

Murphy, Maggie, author.
High-tech DIY projects with microcontrollers / by Maggie Murphy.
    pages cm. — (Maker kids)
Includes index.
ISBN 978-1-4777-6671-2 (library binding) — ISBN 978-1-4777-6677-4 (pbk.) —
ISBN 978-1-4777-6658-3 (6-pack)
1. Microcontrollers—Juvenile literature. 2. Arduino (Programmable controller)—Juvenile literature. I. Title. II. Title: High-tech do-it-yourself projects with microcontrollers.
TJ223.P76M87 2015
629.8'9—dc23
                    2014000742

Manufactured in the United States of America

CPSIA Compliance Information: Batch #WS14PK9: For Further Information contact Rosen Publishing, New York, New York at 1-800-237-9932

Contents

Fun with Microcontrollers

You have probably used a computer to do your homework, play games, or surf the web. Did you know that you have also used a computer to microwave your dinner, turn on a television, or set the temperature on an air conditioner?

When you play with a remote-controlled car, you are using a microcontroller.

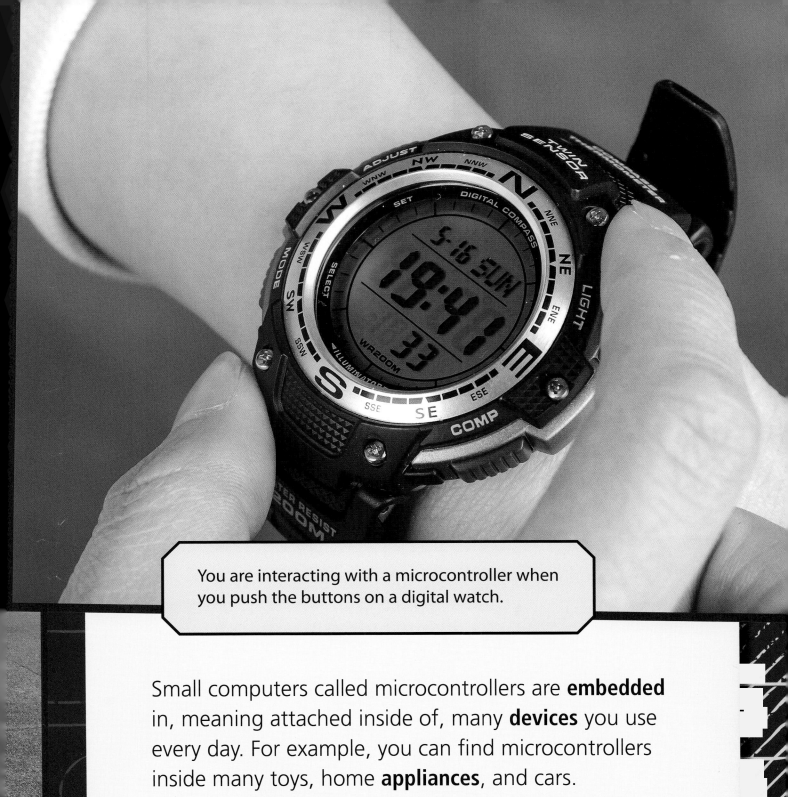

You are interacting with a microcontroller when you push the buttons on a digital watch.

Small computers called microcontrollers are **embedded** in, meaning attached inside of, many **devices** you use every day. For example, you can find microcontrollers inside many toys, home **appliances**, and cars.

You can also program a microcontroller to perform a specific task. Microcontroller projects are a great way to learn about computer programming and electronics. In this book, you will find many fun projects with microcontrollers to try!

History of the Microcontroller

The history of the microcontroller starts with the **microprocessor**. A microprocessor is a computer chip that is able to **process** many different kinds of instructions, even at the same time. A microprocessor is powerful, but by itself it is useless. It must be connected to other things like memory and **input** and **output** devices in order to do anything.

Microprocessors may be small, but they are powerful and can run many cool devices.

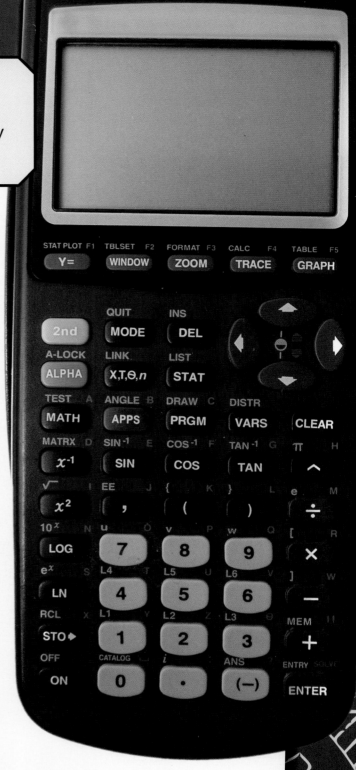

Many kids have learned how to program the microprocessors in their graphing calculators so they can also play games on them.

Microprocessors were developed in the 1970s. The first ones were built for electronic calculators. By the early 1990s, microprocessors could be found in home computers and portable devices such as cell phones, pagers, and the Nintendo Game Boy.

It would be too expensive to put a microprocessor and all the parts it needs to work into many electronic devices. The need for a cheaper processor is where the idea for the microcontroller came from.

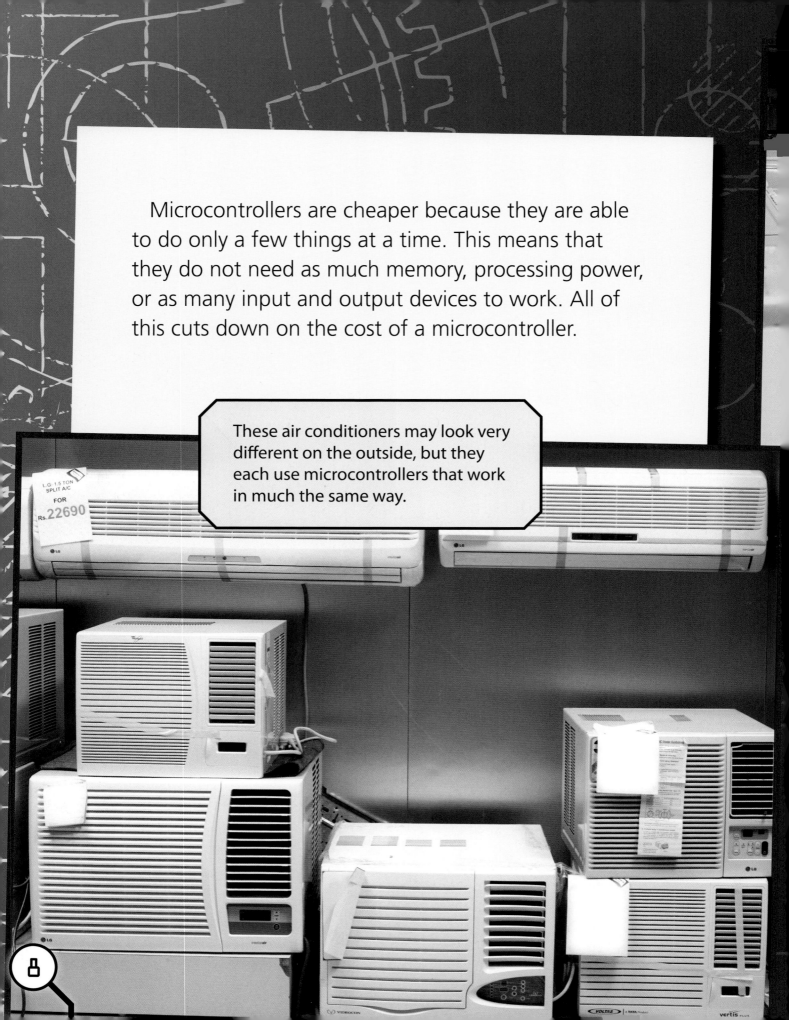

Microcontrollers are cheaper because they are able to do only a few things at a time. This means that they do not need as much memory, processing power, or as many input and output devices to work. All of this cuts down on the cost of a microcontroller.

These air conditioners may look very different on the outside, but they each use microcontrollers that work in much the same way.

Microcontrollers are hidden in many devices you use every day. For example, most refrigerators have microcontrollers.

Microcontrollers in Toys

You can find microcontrollers inside of many **interactive** toys. If a toy talks when you squeeze it, moves when you press a button, or works with a remote control, it probably has a microcontroller inside. The microcontroller runs your input through a program that makes output so that the toy will talk or move.

Bigger is not always better. Microcontrollers may not be able to do as much as microprocessors, but they are perfect for devices that only need to do a few things. You can find microcontrollers in many home appliances such as dishwashers, thermostats, air conditioners, televisions, and garage door openers. If an appliance has a keypad or uses a remote control, it probably has a microcontroller inside of it.

How Do Microcontrollers Work?

A microcontroller is a small computer. Its job is to gather information from input **components**, process it, and then send signals to output components that will perform some kind of action. There are many different kinds of microcontrollers, but they all have similarities. For example, every microcontroller will have input and output pins, a central processing unit (CPU), and memory.

You can't see the many parts of a microcontroller because they are kept inside of a casing.

Modern cars use microcontrollers to unlock doors, start engines, blow up airbags, and more.

Microcontrollers are generally embedded in larger electronic devices. These devices have input components such as **sensors**, touchscreens, or keypads. These components connect with things on the microcontroller called input pins. When you interact with an input component, information is sent through the input pins to the microcontroller's CPU.

The CPU is the microcontroller's brain. It processes input with help from the programs stored in the microcontroller's memory. When it finishes processing the input, the CPU sends new information through output pins to the connected output components. An output component can be anything that produces sound, motion, light, or anything else.

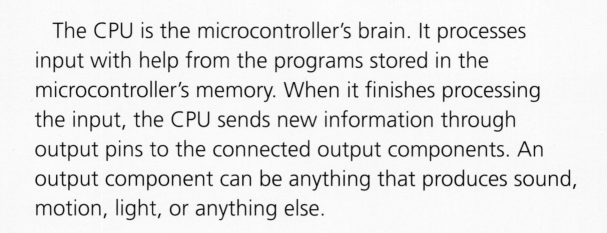
The buttons you push on a microwave send input to its microcontroller.

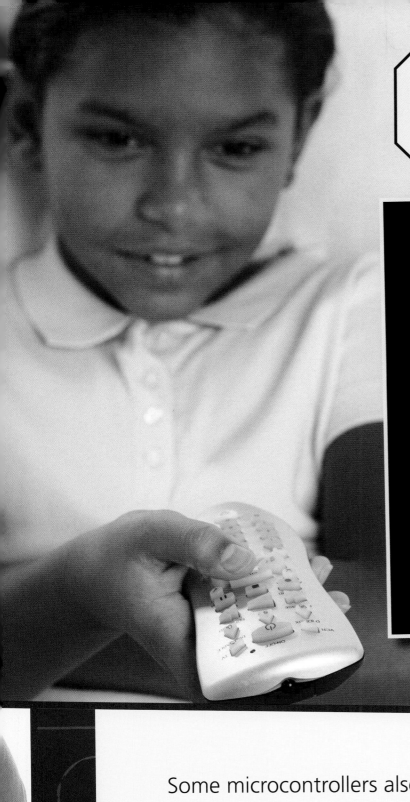

The infrared signal that a remote control uses is actually a kind of light that humans cannot see.

Remote Controls

Remote controls are another kind of input component. When you press a button on a remote control, it sends an **infrared** signal to a sensor in an electronic device. This sensor sends the signal to the device's microcontroller so it can be processed. Think about this the next time you change the channel on a television!

Some microcontrollers also have timers or counters. These allow the microcontroller to perform actions for specific lengths of time. Microcontrollers may also have something called an interrupt control. This helps the microcontroller delay, pause, restart, and stop a task it is performing.

13

Join a Club!

It is fun to experiment with microcontrollers. It's also fun to share your ideas and learn from others. If working with other kids to build microcontroller projects sounds fun, you might want to join a club!

A club is a group whose members all share an interest. Your school or public library might have a science club, electronics club, or robotics club that you could join. In any of these clubs, you can learn about microcontrollers and experiment with different projects. If there are no clubs to join nearby, ask a teacher, librarian, or other adult about starting one!

An electronics club may not always experiment with microcontrollers, but you can use what you learn for your own projects at home.

Combining littleBits

When you do a microcontroller project, you will use other electronic parts, such as sensors and LEDs, to create a **circuit**. A circuit is a chain of electronic devices through which electricity travels. One fun way to learn more about building circuits is by using littleBits.

Each Bit is clearly labeled with its function. Arrows point in the direction that the electricity will move through it.

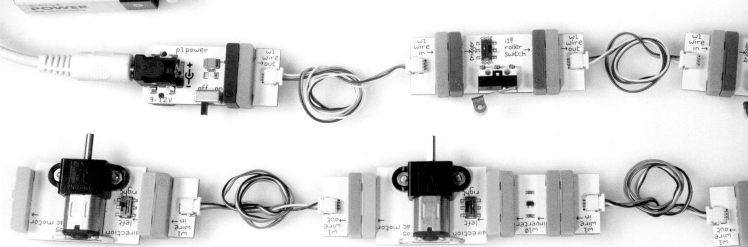

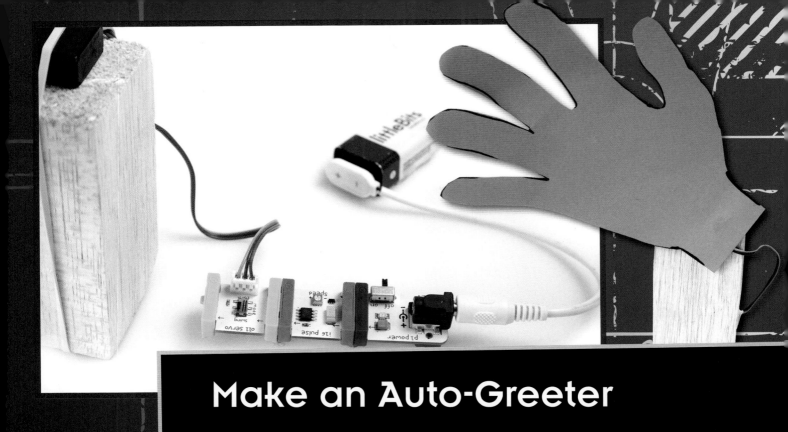

Make an Auto-Greeter

This project is fun and quick. First, connect a USB power Bit to a pulse Bit. Then connect the pulse Bit to a servo Bit. Set the servo Bit to swing mode. Mount the servo Bit on a small wooden or plastic block. Next, use a pencil to trace your hand on a piece of construction paper then use scissors to cut it out. Tape the hand to the servo Bit. Turn on your circuit and watch it wave hello! For a video tutorial, go to littlebits.cc/projects/auto-greeter.

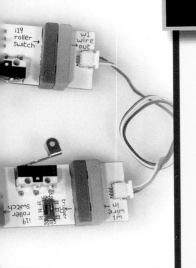

littleBits is a company that makes many different electronic parts, called Bits, that snap together with magnets. There are different kinds of Bits that do specific jobs in building an electronic device. For example, blue Bits supply the power and orange Bits act like wires. Pink Bits gather input, and green Bits do different things to produce output.

littleBits are easy to use because you do not need to program anything. When you experiment by combining different Bits, you will learn about the basics of electronics.

Many kids and adults are making all kinds of things using littleBits. You can find many of these projects at littlebits.cc/projects. You can make them yourself or upload your own projects so others can make them, too! New projects with instructions, pictures, and videos are uploaded often. You can also post comments and ask questions.

The possibilities with littleBits are endless. These Bits are linked together to make music by reading the markings on this paper.

You can combine circuits of Bits with things around the house. This circuit turns on a water cooler to fill a glass for you.

Dreambits

littleBits is constantly adding new kinds of Bits. That doesn't mean you have to sit around and wait for them to think up the new Bit you need, though. Users are encouraged to post the ideas they have for new Bits, nicknamed dreamBits, on the littleBits website. It's a cool way to get involved in the littleBits community. Who knows? Maybe they'll end up making your dreamBit one day.

Getting to Know Arduino™

When you are ready to try a microcontroller project, one of the first things you need to do is find a microcontroller board to work with. A microcontroller board is like a computer chip with many parts you will need for your projects already attached to it and connected together.

Arduino™ makes several kinds of microcontroller boards. They come in many sizes and have different components.

Reset button

Input/output pins

USB connection

Microcontroller

Power supply

Get to know the Arduino™ Uno a little better. The labels in this picture point out the major parts you should know about.

One board that is very easy to use is the Arduino™ Uno. It has free programming software, connects easily to your computer with a USB cord, and is cheap. Arduino™ boards are also great to use because there is troubleshooting help on their website, Arduino.cc, and many free online tutorials.

One easy way to get started with the Arduino™ is to buy a starter kit. Arduino™ makes an official starter kit, which comes with an Arduino™ Uno microcontroller, a bunch of parts, and a projects booklet. You can find this starter kit on the Arduino™ website. You can also purchase other starter kits or the individual parts you will need from other online stores such as Amazon.com, Makershed.com, or Sparkfun.com. You can also try your local Radio Shack or hobby store.

You can have a lot of fun with microcontrollers. If you can dream it up, you can make it happen with the right parts and a little dedication!

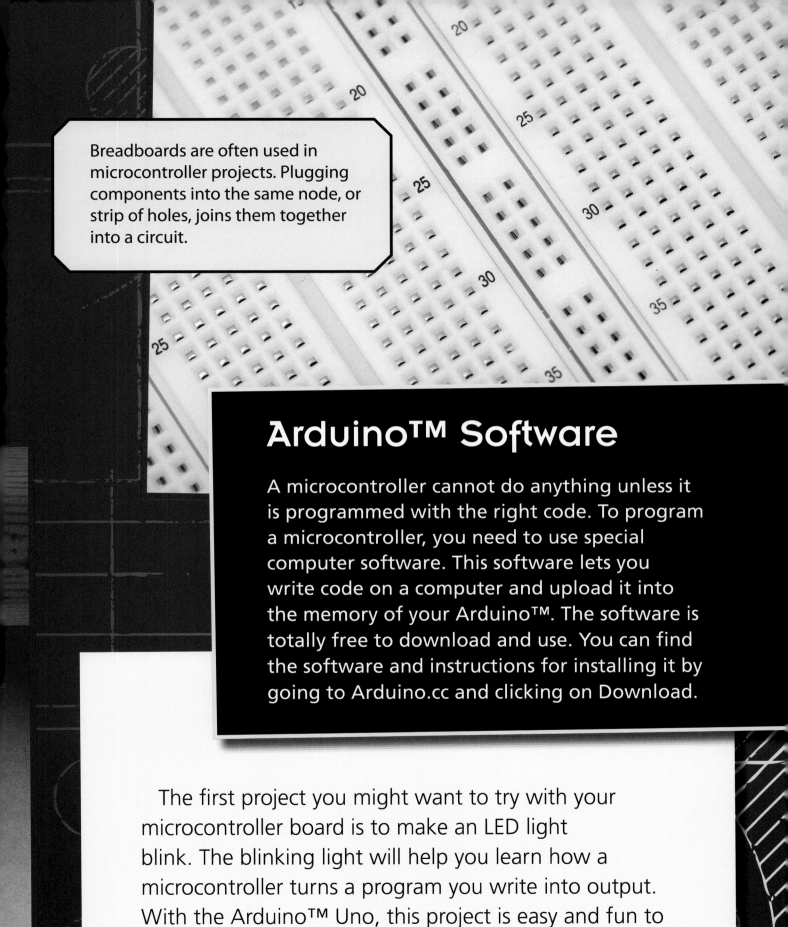

Breadboards are often used in microcontroller projects. Plugging components into the same node, or strip of holes, joins them together into a circuit.

Arduino™ Software

A microcontroller cannot do anything unless it is programmed with the right code. To program a microcontroller, you need to use special computer software. This software lets you write code on a computer and upload it into the memory of your Arduino™. The software is totally free to download and use. You can find the software and instructions for installing it by going to Arduino.cc and clicking on Download.

The first project you might want to try with your microcontroller board is to make an LED light blink. The blinking light will help you learn how a microcontroller turns a program you write into output. With the Arduino™ Uno, this project is easy and fun to experiment with. Turn to the next chapter for directions!

Make It Blink!

For this project, you will need access to a computer that has the Arduino™ software installed on it. Have an adult help you download and install it by going to Arduino.cc and clicking Download.

You will need:

- 1 Arduino™ Uno board
- 1 Arduino™ USB cable
- 1 220-ohm resistor
- 1 LED light
- 1 pair of scissors

1

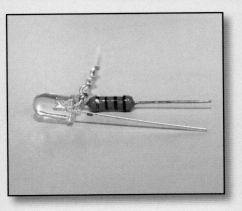

Attach the long leg of the LED to one leg of the resistor by twisting them together. Cut the other leg of the resistor so it and the short leg of the LED are even.

2

Put the straight leg of the resistor into pin 13 on the Arduino™ board and the cut leg of the LED into the GND (ground) pin.

Plug the Arduino™ into your computer with the USB cord.

Start the Arduino™ software and enter the code found online at Arduino.cc/en/Tutorial/Blink under Code. Click Upload.

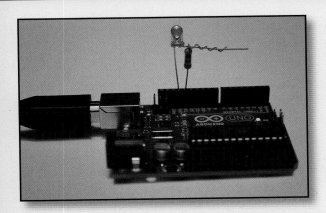

Once the code has been uploaded, the LED light will blink on for 1 second and then turn off for 1 second. It will continue to do this until you turn off or reset the Arduino™.

You can also make the LED blink in different patterns. Just add more lines of code and change the lengths of the delays. Remember that HIGH turns on the LED, LOW turns it off, and a delay of 1000 equals 1 second. See the example to the right for a longer code and explanations for each line of code.

```
void loop() {
  digitalWrite(led, HIGH);   // turns the LED on
    delay(1000);             // waits for 1 second
  digitalWrite(led, LOW);    // turns the LED off
    delay(1500);             // waits for 1.5 seconds
  digitalWrite(led, HIGH);   // turns the LED on
    delay(2000);             // waits for 2 seconds
  digitalWrite(led, LOW);    // turns the LED off
    delay(500);              // waits for .5 second
```

More Arduino™ Projects

Making an LED light blink is just the very beginning of what you can do with a microcontroller. The next paragraphs describe some fun projects. Links to them can be found in the Projects Links box at the end of this chapter. Many other projects can also be found online.

Some advanced projects require soldering. Soldering joins two things together using melted metal. This makes a strong connection when it cools.

The LEDs and resistor in this picture have been soldered, or joined with liquid metal, to a circuit board.

Makezine.com is a great place to find new electronics projects, many of which use an Arduino™ board. Take your experimenting with LEDs even further by learning how to change the color of an RGB (red-green-blue) LED.

Instructables.com is known for posting all kinds of maker projects. They have tons that use the Arduino™. One of them teaches you how to use a breadboard to make a cool electronic die.

Projects Links

RGB LED – Makezine.com/projects/use-a-common-anode-rgb-led/
Electronic Die – Instructables.com/id/Arduino-Project-E-Dice-Beginner/?ALLSTEPS!

Just the Beginning!

Experimenting with microcontrollers and electronic devices is super fun. There are endless projects for you to try. Once you have the basics of programming a microcontroller down, there are so many things you can do. Try building a robot or playing with a microprocessor such as the Raspberry Pi!

If there's something you'd like to make, see if you can figure out how to do it. You may need to try a few times, but that's how you learn.

Countless kids around the country and world are building all kinds of amazing things. Join in!

All around the world, kids are taking part in the do-it-yourself maker movement. This means they are learning how to build high-tech projects themselves. Microcontroller projects are just one small part of this movement. Find more projects online, connect with others, join a club, and keep building!

More About Making

Check out the lists below for more ways to learn about microcontrollers and microcontroller projects. You can also ask an adult to help you use the library and search the Internet for other projects, books, and stores!

Books

Boxall, John. *Arduino Workshop: A Hands-On Introduction with 65 Projects*. San Francisco: No Starch Press, 2013.

Monk, Simon. *30 Arduino Projects for the Evil Genius*. Second ed. New York: McGraw-Hill/TAB Electronics, 2013.

Websites

- For Arduino™ tips, help, and projects, visit Arduino.cc.
- Learn about another popular microcontroller board at Raspberrypi.org.
- Sylvia, a young maker, posts fun video tutorials at Sylviashow.com.

Parts and Kits

Arduino.cc
Browndoggadgets.com
Makershed.com
Sparkfun.com

Glossary

appliances (uh-PLY-ents-ez) Machines designed to do specific things.

circuit (SER-ket) The complete path of an electric current.

components (kum-POH-nents) Parts used to make something else.

devices (dih-VYS-ez) Machines that are made for special purposes.

embedded (em-BED-ed) Attached inside of something.

infrared (in-fruh-RED) A type of light that humans cannot see.

input (IN-puht) Information that is received by a device.

interactive (in-ter-AK-tiv) Able to respond or to change when played with.

microprocessor (MY-kroh-PRAH-seh-sur) A computer chip that handles input and output.

output (OWT-puht) Something produced by an action.

process (PRAH-ses) To change something using a special series of steps.

sensors (SEN-sorz) Devices that gather information to be processed.

Index

A
air conditioner(s), 4, 9
appliance(s), 5, 9

B
button, 9, 13

C
chip, 6, 20
component(s), 10–13
computer(s), 4–5, 7, 10,
  21, 23–25

D
device(s), 5–9, 11, 13,
  16–17, 28

E
electronics, 5, 18

K
keypad(s), 9, 11
kind(s), 6, 10, 13,
  17–19, 27

M
memory, 6, 8, 10,
  12, 23
microprocessor(s), 6–7,
  9, 28

P
part(s), 7, 16–17,
  20, 22, 29

ports, 10–12
power, 8, 17
programming, 5
program(s), 9,
  12, 23

R
remote control(s), 9, 13

S
sensor(s), 11, 13, 16

T
task, 5, 13
television(s), 4, 9, 13
temperature, 4
toy(s), 5, 9

Websites

Due to the changing nature of Internet links, PowerKids Press has developed an online list of websites related to the subject of this book. This site is updated regularly. Please use this link to access the list: www.powerkidslinks.com/maker/micro/